fIVE
MEDIEVAL
DANCES

FIVE MEDIEVAL DANCES

Arranged by

Samuel Milligan

for small Harp
with optional instruments
Recorders (or Flutes), Hand Drum (or Tambourine), Tenor Drum,
Finger Cymbals, and Hurdy–Gurdy (or Viola)

Ars Musicæ Hispaniæ

a division of

WingsPress

San Antonio, Texas

2019

On the Cover:

Three harps by Lynne Lewandowski, Bellows Falls, VT, left to right:
Harp after painting by Hieronymus Bosch, c. 1495.
Harp modeled on an 11ᵗʰ/12ᵗʰ Century English harp depicted in a manuscript from
Abbot Gerbert, St. Blasius Monastery, Germany.
Dog-headed harp after an illustration in the *Cantigas* of Alfonso el Sabio.

In rear, hurdy-gurdy by Altarwind, O'Brien, OR (with modifications):
In front, hand drum and tambourine, unknown makers, resting on tambourine,
thick finger cymbals (crotales) by Avedis Zildjean, Norwell, MA.

Frontis page illustration: 11ᵗʰ/12ᵗʰ Century English harp from a manuscript from
Abbot Gerbert, St. Blasius Monastery, Germany. From Galpin, Francis W.,
Old English Instruments of Music, Methuen & Co., London, 1932, p. 8. Image reversed.
Elsewhere: Two hurdy-gurdy players redrawn from the
Cantigas de Santa Maria, No. 160, Escorial Codex j.b.2, plate 154v.

First Edition

Paper Edition ISBN: 978-1-60940-609-7

Ebook editions:
ISBN: 978-1-60940-610-3

Wings Press
San Antonio, Texas, and elsewhere.
wingspresspublishing@gmail.com

All Wings Press titles are distributed to the trade by
Independent Publishers Group
www.ipgbook.com

for

Gordon Johnston

Superb musician—harpist, organist, arranger, composer and conductor, with gratitude for all the help he has been, not only with solid musical advice, but with bringing me into the world of musical typesetting

CONTENTS

IF YOU DON'T OWN THE
MEDIEVAL INSTRUMENTS CALLED FOR.....

Feel free to use modern substitutes. While an authentic reproduction of a medieval harp is ideal, most modern lap harps or lever harps can stand in. And in a pinch, even (gasp) pedal harp. The percussions are readily available, substituting the hand drum with a tambourine, if need be, and the hurdy-gurdy can be replaced by a viola, taking care to avoid vibrato for a more authentic sound. And a bit of searching can generally find a recorder player these days. If not, flute will do nicely for soprano recorder, and piccolo flute for sopranino.

The main thing is not to allow the lack of authentic instruments to deny you the knowledge and enjoyment of the music.

Note: Phrase marks are added for ease in reading, and fingerings are only suggestions. Change them to fit your hand as you will.

PROLEGOMENON

Ouring the Middle Ages, literacy, particularly musical literacy, was in the hands of the Church, primarily with the monastic clergy. Naturally, they had little interest in secular music, so little of it was written down. So I like to believe that the few secular melodies that survived represent some of the more popular pieces, the lesser ones being thought unworthy of being preserved.

In any case, what we have can be useful in bringing some variety to a recital. In fact, it would be a splendid idea to alternate these pieces with the songs in the companion book *Seven Medieval Songs for Small Harp with Optional Instruments.*

Never forget that the worst sin you can commit is to bore your audience. Variety will stop that problem in its tracks.

There is very little in the way of ensemble music published these days for small harps, which deprives their owners of all the fun of playing with others. So gather some like-minded friends and put together your own medieval shindig / hèsta / céilí / fête. As I wrote in the notes for the companion medieval songbook:

"You can imagine yourself in the days when knighthood was flourishing, all men brave and all damsels lovely. Fearless Robin Hood, beautiful Maid Marion, dauntless Richard Lionheart, faithful Will Scarlet and their colorful colleagues will be great company, as you, armed with your trusty harp, turn your swashbuckling musical armament against the feckless Sherriff of Nottingham, perfidious Prince John and others cut from the same naughty cloth.

Lubricating the occasion with a jug of mead might be authentic, but will become increasingly counterproductive as the evening passes. A nice cold pitcher of iced tea is a better choice. Serve it in Tyrolean steins and pass it off as a different kind of dark ale."

And call forth the dancers!

Samuel Milligan
Brooklyn, New York
May Day, 2018

Two hurdy-gurdy players redrawn from the
Cantigas de Santa María, No. 160,
Escorial Codex j.b.2, plate 154v.

FIVE
MEDIEVAL DANCES

Full Scores

Danse Royale

French Estampie from Le Manuscrit du Roi

Paris, Bibl. Nat. fr 844. f.5r

Arranged by
Samuel Milligan

Anonymous
13th Century

Danse Royale

Danse Royale

Danse Royale

According to the 14th century Parisian musical theorist Johannes de Grocheo, the estampie consisted of repeated sections, called "pars," or "punctas." We have no idea how the estampie was danced, It is tempting to assume from the name that it was some sort of stamping dance, but the definition in the Oxford English Dictionary says that the word derives from a Provençal original, meaning "to resound."

It also appears under the names "estampida," "estampita," or in Latin "stantipes."

Estampie Real

La Quinte Estampie Real from Le Manuscrit du Roi

Paris, Bibl. Nat. fr 844, f.104v

Arranged by
Samuel Milligan

Mid 13th Century
Anonymous

Estampie Real

Estampie Real

Estampie Real

Lamento di Tristano

Italian Estampie
Brit. Lib. Add. Ms 29987

Edited by
Samuel Milligan

Anonymous, 14th Century

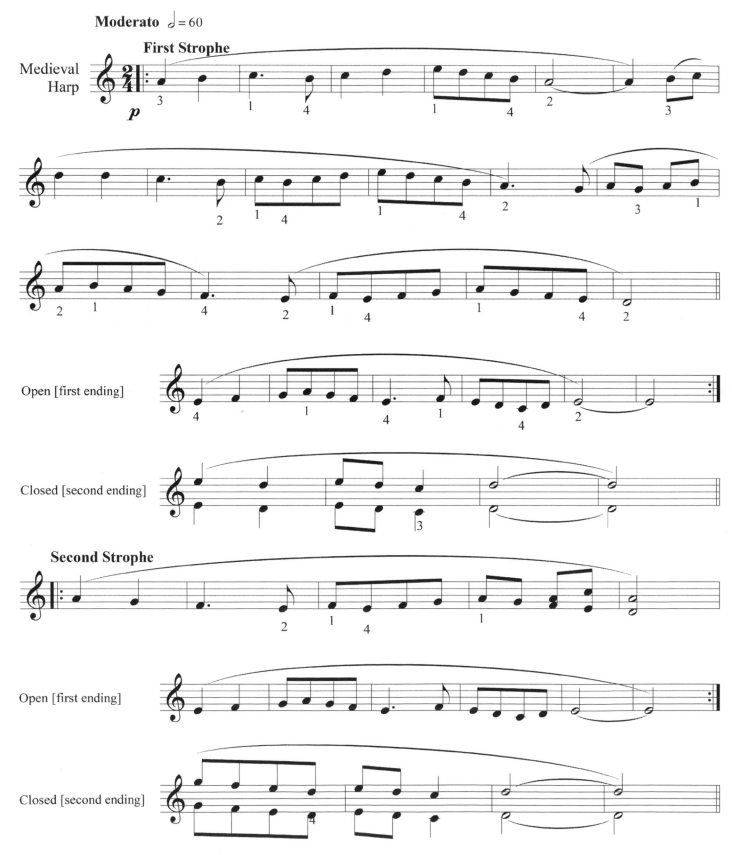

Lamento di Tristano

Third Strophe

Open [first ending]

Closed [second ending]

rit.

Among his other talents, Tristan was an accomplished harpist. The story of his love affair with Iseult is one of the most tragic in all literature, known all over Medieval Europe--even in Italy, as we see here.

This piece is, technically, an estampie, and as such is meant to be danced at a vigorous tempo. It is followed by a faster rotta in the manuscript. [See next page.] The two should be played in tandem. If, however, the estampie is too fast, the effect of contrast is lost. I prefer to ignore the dance idea entirely, and play it much more slowly than the tempo given here. I suspect it might have been a true lament, speeded up to make it danceable. It is, after all, a lament.

Note that each strophe has two endings, one open, and one closed. The open ending has a half cadence, and the closed ending has a full cadence. Both endings for the third strophe are missing from the manuscript, so I have repeated those from the first strophe.

La Rotta

Edited by
Samuel Milligan

Anonymoous, 14th Century
Brit. Lib. Add. Ms. 29987

La Rotta

Czaldy Waldy

Two Late Medieval Dance Tunes
Cz. Nat. Lib. Ms. xvii f-9

Arranged by
Samuel Milligan

14th or 15th Century Bohemia

Czaldy Waldy

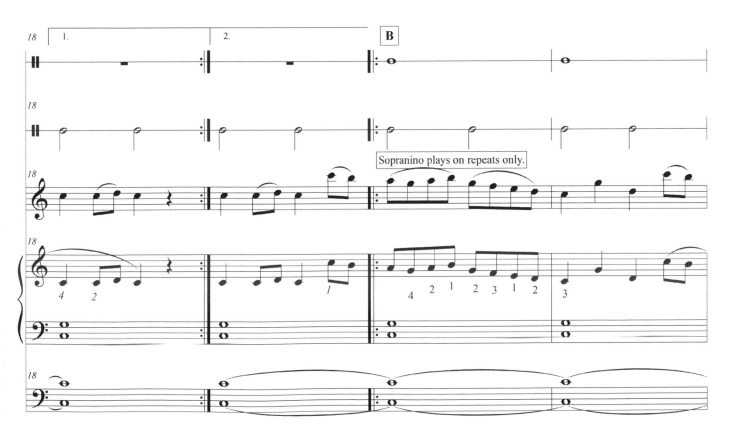

Sopranino plays on repeats only.

Czaldy Waldy

(1 min. 38 sec.)

The name Czaldy Waldy is attached to the second of two pieces found on the same manuscript. (B)
The first (A) is lacking a title.

What the title means is unknown, but since there is no text, I assume them to be instrumental
dances, and with such a peppy title, seem to demand an allegro tempo, as does the music itself.

According to the Czech scholar Václav Plocek, neither of the pieces can be accurately dated, but
late 14th or early 15 century seems likely.

King David and his musicians depicted in an eleventh century Anglo Saxon manuscript.

Harp Parts

Estampie Real

Arranged by
Samuel Milligan

La Quinte Estampie Real from Le Manuscrit du Roi

Paris, Bibl. Nat. fr 844, f.104v

Mid 13th Century
Anonymous

Estampie Real

Czaldy Waldy

Arranged by
Samuel Milligan

Two Late Medieval Dance Tunes
Cz. Nat. Lib. Ms. xvii f-9

14th or 15th Century Bohemia

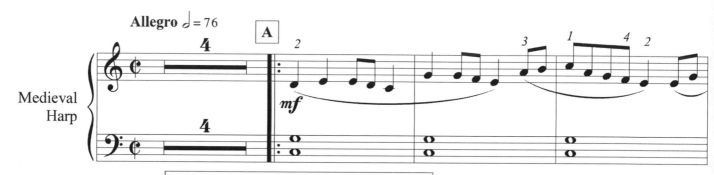

Medieval
Harp

Left hand may be omitted if using a smaller harp.

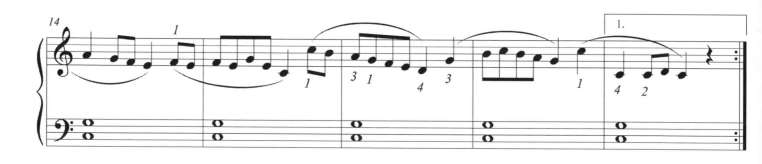

Czaldy Waldy

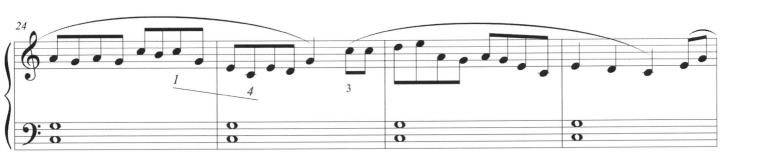

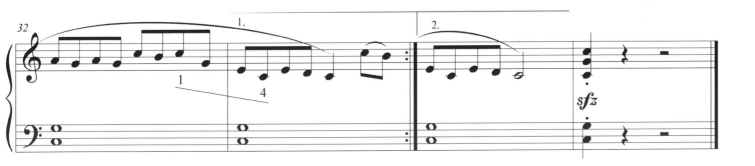

Danse Royale

French Estampie from Le Manuscrit du Roi

Paris, Bibl. Nat. fr 844. f.5r

Arranged by
Samuel Milligan

Anonymous
13th Century

Recorder Parts

Estampie Real

La Quinte Estampie Real from Le Manuscrit du Roi

Paris, Bibl. Nat. fr 844, f.104v

Arranged by
Samuel Milligan

Mid 13th Century
Anonymous

Czaldy Waldy

Two Late Medieval Dance Tunes
Cz. Nat. Lib. Ms. xvii f-9

Arranged by
Samuel Milligan

14th or 15th Century Bohemia

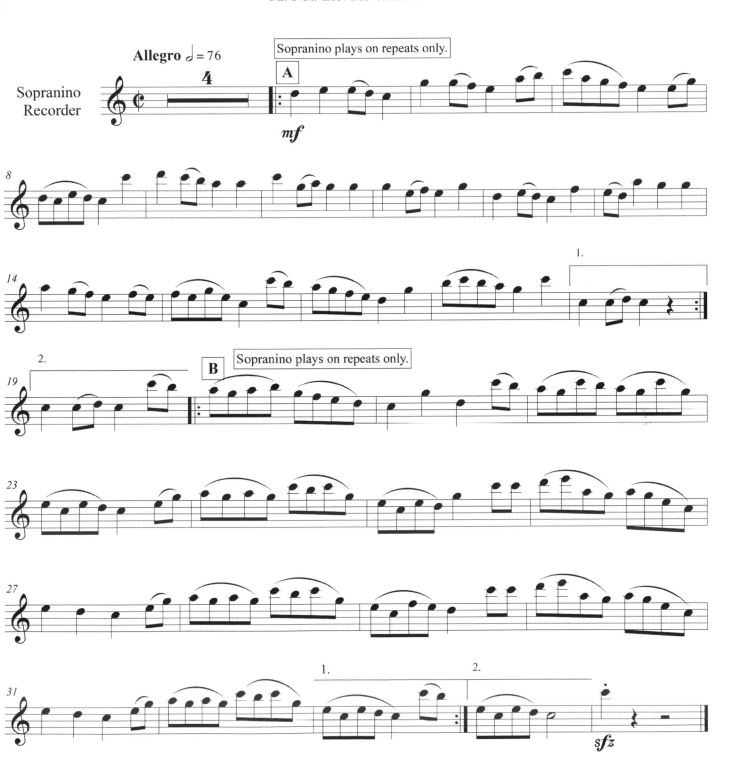

Danse Royale

French Estampie from Le Manuscrit du Roi

Paris, Bibl. Nat. fr 844. f.5r

Arranged by
Samuel Milligan

Anonymous
13th Century

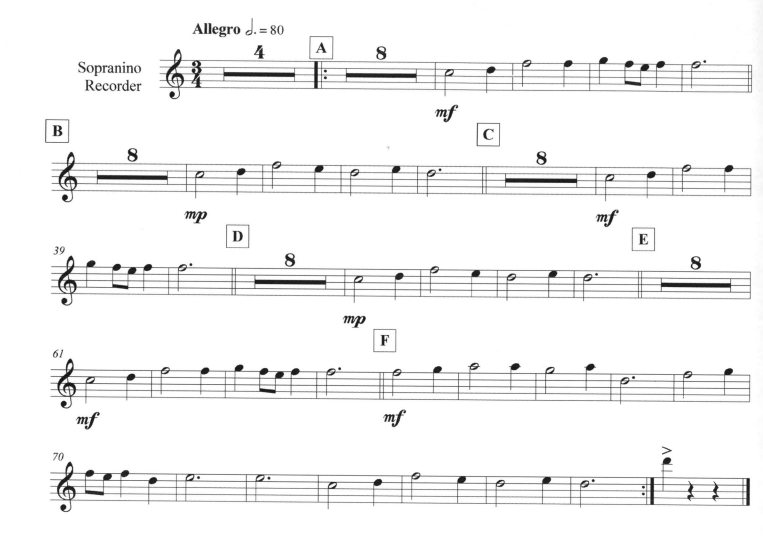

Finger Cymbals

Estampie Real

La Quinte Estampie Real from Le Manuscrit du Roi

Paris, Bibl. Nat. fr 844, f.104v

Arranged by
Samuel Milligan

Mid 13th Century
Anonymous

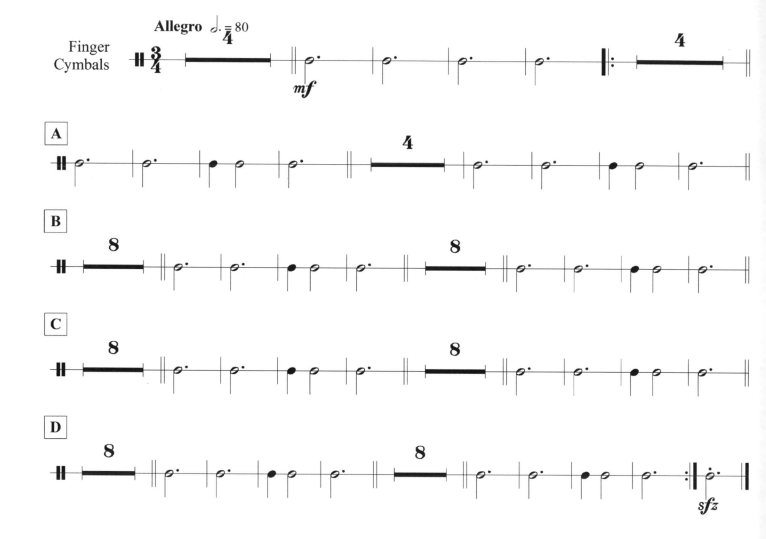

The name of Samuel Milligan is one of the first that the beginning harp student is likely to encounter. When the harp making firm Lyon & Healy introduced their new Troubadour lever harp in 1961, they commissioned Milligan to furnish a new method, *Fun From the First,* plus another collection of pieces, *Medieval to Modern.* These have become standard repertory for harp students, and many pieces can be found as required material for harp contests and festivals. The introduction of the Troubadour harp and the publication of Milligan's music have been responsible, in large part, for the beginnings of the renaissance in harp playing that we see today. Where there was once little music for lever harp, there is now an abundance. Where there was only one maker of lever harps, there are now many.

Samuel Milligan on the cover of *The American Harp Journal,* Summer 2017.

Born in 1932 near Joplin, Missouri, Milligan grew up in the Texas Panhandle. Even though sprung from such unlikely beginnings, his life was always defined by music. Both parents were enthusiastic singers, and he began piano lessons at age nine. However, his musical life began in earnest when he acquired a Clark Irish harp, which naturally fit the plans of his Irish father.

Harp scholarships allowed him to attend Del Mar Junior College in Corpus Christi, Texas, where he encountered his first real harp teacher, LaVerne Hodges Peterson, who installed a solid technique. He later transferred to North Texas State College (now the University of North Texas) where he received a Bachelor of Music degree with a major in harp performance. He began a master's degree in musicology, working with Dr. Helen Hewitt, who further fueled his fascination with early music, an interest first developed when he was in high school. However, the next year found him employed as a harp technician by Lyon & Healy in their New York City showroom. This enabled him to explore many avenues of harp playing, such as being a substitute on Broadway and at Radio City Music Hall, as well as much single-date playing, and a national tour with a chamber orchestra for Columbia Artists Management.

In the meantime, he began studies with Laura Newell, who had been Toscanini's first choice as harpist for his NBC Symphony. Milligan was impressed by her superb technique and musicianship. Among other things, she stressed economy of motion and careful finger placement to avoid any sibilants.

In 1967, at the request of Lucien Thomson, president of the American Harp Society, Milligan became the founding editor of the *American Harp Journal*, serving until 1971, afterwards contributing articles from time to time. He later served on the Boards of the American Harp Society and the Historical Harp Society, and was appointed by the AHS as a liaison between the two groups.

Since 2000, he has indulged his love for early Spanish music, an interest that had been encouraged years before by Nicanor Zabaleta, the Spanish harp virtuoso. For many years he organized various conjuntos for the performance of this music, the repertory covering the Medieval, Renaissance and Baroque periods, with emphasis on the music of the Spanish colonial New World. This involves much music for strictly diatonic harps, which Milligan defends by making a comparison to visual art, saying: "In the same way that a black and white drawing by Leonardo da Vinci is no less great art than any of his paintings in color, so a diatonic piece of music can be as artistically significant as something chromatic. In fact, economy of means can add to its artistic value."

Milligan has been the recipient of two recent awards. One, in 2008 from the American Harp Society, honors his outstanding service to the AHS and to the harp. Another, presented by the Somerset Harp Festival in 2014, is in honor of his lifetime achievement.

He currently lives in Brooklyn, New York, surrounded by harps of all sizes and descriptions.

Other titles by
Samuel Milligan

For lever or pedal harp

Fun From the First (a method in two volumes)

Medieval to Modern (repertory in three volumes)

Der Jolly Huntsman und der Kuckoo (for piccolo, harp and shotgun [slapstick])

Vox Cœlestis (five pieces for harp and organ)

Nine Sephardic Songs (for harp and voice)

Seven Medieval Songs (for harp and voice)

For pedal harp

Vox Angelica (four pieces for harp and organ)

Black and White Rag by George Botsford

Kol Nidrei by Max Bruch (for cello, harp and organ)

Choral

Campanas de Belén / Bells of Bethlehem (for SATB choir and organ
with optional harp, handbells and glockenspiel)

Wings Press was founded in 1975 by Joanie Whitebird and Joseph F. Lomax, both deceased, as "an informal association of artists and cultural mythologists dedicated to the preservation of the literature of the nation of Texas." Publisher, editor and designer since 1995, Bryce Milligan is honored to carry on and expand that mission to include the finest in American writing—meaning all of the Americas, without commercial considerations clouding the decision to publish or not to publish.

Wings Press intends to produce multi-cultural books, chapbooks, ebooks, recordings and broadsides that enlighten the human spirit and enliven the mind. Everyone ever associated with Wings has been or is a writer, and we know well that writing is a transformational art form capable of changing the world, primarily by allowing us to glimpse something of each other's souls. We believe that good writing is innovative, insightful, and interesting. But most of all it is honest. As Bob Dylan put it, "To live outside the law, you must be honest."

Likewise, Wings Press is committed to treating the planet itself as a partner. Thus the press uses as much recycled material as possible, from the paper on which the books are printed to the boxes in which they are shipped.

As Robert Dana wrote in *Against the Grain*, "Small press publishing is personal publishing. In essence, it's a matter of personal vision, personal taste and courage, and personal friendships." Welcome to our world.

Colophon

This first edition of *Five Medieval Dances*, by Samuel Milligan, has been printed on 60 pound paper containing a percentage of recycled fiber. Titles have been set in Scotford Uncial and Pendragon FLF type, the text in Adobe Caslon type. This book was designed by Bryce Milligan.

Wings Press titles are distributed to the trade by the
Independent Publishers Group
www.ipgbook.com
and in Europe by Gazelle
www.gazellebookservices.co.uk

Also available as an ebook.